I DON'T LIKE IT… BUT MAYBE

JULIA NOBLE SIVARAJAH

This book is dedicated to my wonderful children, Esme and Nolan, who continue to be inspirations for my works.

I don't like it when I can't put on my shoes.
Is it the right way? I keep getting confused!
I feel frustrated.

But maybe…
**I can put on fun stickers to
remind myself!
Practice makes perfect, and it's
okay to get help.**

I don't like it when my
brother takes my toys.
He is not sharing even
when I use my polite voice!
I become angry.

But maybe...
**I will play with something else
and wait my turn.
He is still a baby, I can teach him sharing
and help him learn!**

I don't like it when I'm told to
go to bed.
I am not done playing yet
and want more fun instead!
I am disappointed.

But maybe…
**I can think of exciting things to
do when I wake.
If I go to sleep soon,
I can get up early to bake!**

I don't like it when there are too
many vegetables to eat.
They are not tasty,
I wish I could just have more treats!
I feel disgusted.

But maybe...
**I can mix these in with other yummy
things on my plate.
I will probably get stronger since
this is what superheroes ate!**

I don't like it when I need to learn
something hard.
I would rather watch TV
or play outside in my backyard!
I am nervous.

But maybe…
**If I use my favorite colors the work
will be more fun.
I can get smarter and still enjoy
with my friends when I am done!**

ADDITION
86 + 10 = [96]
54 + 13 = [67]
91 + 8 = [99]
16 + 41 = [57]
72 + 12 = [84]
SUBTRACTION
35 - 44 = [ ]
28 - 60 = [ ]
- 30 = [ ]
57 = [ ]

I don't like it when I am told to clean up my stuff.
There is too big of a mess, and it is going to be tough!
I feel overwhelmed.

But maybe…
**While I clean there can be treasures
to hunt for?
Cleaning can be rewarding because
I can find toys I lost before!**

So, when I don't like
something, it doesn't have
to be a bad day.
Because I can always
try to think of a
"BUT MAYBE" way!

THE END

Acknowledgments

Thank you to my spouse, family, and friends that encourage and support me every step of the way.

About the Author

Julia is a Registered Psychotherapist in Toronto,
Canada. She is dedicated to helping children, youth,
and adults with mental health and/or addiction issues in enhancing
their well-being and improving their quality of life. She holds a Master's Degree
in Counseling Psychology and a Bachelor's Degree in Psychology.
Julia is also the author of the children's book, "When I feel My Tough Feelings".
In addition, she is a mother of two little ones within a family of passionate
readers, who are her biggest fans!

Made in the USA
Monee, IL
07 July 2026